Up All Night

an anthology of short plays

by

Gregory Crafts

www.gregorycrafts.com
www.theatreunleashed.com

UP ALL NIGHT

Copyright © 2012, Gregory Crafts

To Jenn,

Thank you for being my rock and my inspiration.

Contents

INTRODUCTION

"The greater the obstacle, the more glory in overcoming it." - Moliere

The concept seems simple enough. At sunset, give a writer a prompt, a number of characters and a 9 AM deadline. Hand the resulting script over to a team of players that rehearse it all day and put the show up in front of a live audience that night. Sounds so easy, you'd think anyone can do it. However, like most things in life, this is a lot harder you think. It's a creative challenge not to be taken lightly, but one that can be quite rewarding if you are up to the task. In the end, if you rise to the occasion, you're left with something you can be proud of for a lifetime.

I think that's part of the allure – the simplicity of the concept. It gives you a false sense of security, almost like a warm blanket that you wrap around yourself, and from within its cozy folds you find it all too easy to say "sure, what the hell? I'll do it" when your producer asks if you want to write for the next show. It's quite the cold jolt when you get your prompt and your character list and you realize you have no idea what you're going to do with them. At that point, it's already too late. There's no backing out, because there's a team of people depending on you to cough up a script by morning so they can share it with a paying audience that night. Oh, and it better be good. No pressure.

To date, I've taken that chance seven different times. Some of the stories have come quickly and easily for me. Others have kept me up until after sunrise, chugging pot after pot of coffee all night long and cursing my arrogance for thinking that I could do this again. There are times I remember staring at my laptop, bleary-eyed and barely lucid. The words on the screen blurry, my brain fighting to remember their meaning. Somehow, I clawed and struggled…and eventually the story emerged.

It's an intense process. With so little time to develop your script, you're forced to make quick decisions. You tell your story in ways you wouldn't normally consider because it's the only idea you've got and there's no time for second-guessing. You write with your gut, edit as you go and hope you're awake enough to catch any embarrassing typos. You make it work. In the end, you send it off, exhausted and vaguely wondering if what you came up with will be good (or even comprehendible) to anyone besides your sleep-deprived self.

I don't think there's a single script in here that I didn't apologize to our producer for when I sent it in. That sounds like a strange thing to admit now, in the foreword of an anthology that I'm very proud of, but it's true. My preemptive apologies were an honest, almost reflexive, reaction to the possibility of failure. There's always a very real fear when working under these conditions that you will write something that is just plain bad, or worse, you won't be able to write anything at all. That fear has always been my biggest obstacle in these undertakings and I've learned that you can fight it by making strong choices, taking bold chances and having a sense of humor with your writing. Even still, it's impossible to eliminate every shred of doubt you'll feel before seeing your work on its feet in front of an audience. In the end, you have to accept that this is a terrifying process, but trust me when I say it's worth it. This anthology is very real evidence of just how rewarding it can be.

So with that, I proudly present to you six one-act plays of varying lengths between five and fifteen minutes. They were written in one night apiece. To date, they have each been performed exactly once. I hope you enjoy reading them and can find them useful. More importantly, I hope they'll inspire you to take your own chances and challenge yourself. Geronimo.

Gregory Crafts
10/26/11

Up All Night

LIQUID COURAGE

Liquid Courage premiered on February 6th, 2010 as a part of Theatre Unleashed's 24-Hour Theatre Festival, *Love, Sex, Beer and Rock 'n' Roll: A Day in the Life of Cupid*. It featured Carlos Martinez as Tom, David Shackelford as Dick, Tracey Collins as Harriet and Darren T. Mangler as the Waiter. Directed by R. Benito Cardenas. Stage Manager Erin Scott.

LIQUID COURAGE

<u>Setting</u>

A dive bar in North Hollywood, CA. Present day.

<u>Cast</u>

TOM – *Single guy with a secret, 30's.*

DICK – *Tom's best friend. Alpha male. Single guy, 30's.*

HARRIET – *A hooker. 30's.*

WAITER – *Any gender/age. Typical server.*

<u>Scene</u>

Tom and Dick are seated together at a table. Tom sits on the SR side, Dick the UC. An empty chair sits on the SL side of the table.

DICK: So, yeah, man... what's been going on?

TOM: Not much. Y'know... the usual.

DICK: The usual?

TOM: Yeah.

DICK: I used to know what "the usual" was with you. What is it now?

TOM: What do you mean?

DICK: Well, ever since you and Penny broke up, you've been, y'know, different.

TOM: Different.

DICK: Yeah. Different. *(beat)* Like you… I dunno... You're... down, dude.

TOM: So?

DICK: So? So? C'mon bro. This isn't like you. You'd never let losing a chick stop you before. I remember when you broke up with Sharon, you started tappin' Crystal the next night. After that, it was Amy, then Tanya, then Michelle, then...

TOM: Mmm... Michelle.

DICK: That's more like it. Maybe you should give her a call.

TOM: Nah, not so much. She's got someone.

DICK: Really.

TOM: Yeah.

DICK: Serious?

TOM: Serious enough.

DICK: How serious is that?

TOM: Married.

DICK: So?

TOM: Dude.

DICK: C'mon bro. Like you'd let that stop you.

TOM: Well, maybe it would.

DICK: Oh, no. Not you.

TOM: Not me?

DICK: Nah, you're a dog lookin' for a good bone.

TOM: Not anymore.

DICK: No way.

TOM: Yes way.

DICK: A zebra doesn't change its spots... and you, you just need to get back up on that zebra and ride her tight ass to glory.

TOM: *(beat)* What are you talking about?

DICK: You need to find a chick.

TOM: I don't think so.

DICK: I do think so.

TOM: No.

DICK: Yes.

TOM: Dick, you don't understand.

DICK: What's there to understand?

TOM: People change, man. Priorities change.

DICK: Since when is spunkin' up the sheets with something young, hot and tasty not a priority?

TOM: Well, that's always a priority... but tastes... evolve.

DICK: So, no more blondes? Lemme guess. Redheads? Asians? MILFs? You're a little too long in the tooth to be cougar bait, bro.

TOM: Dude, I'm not looking for a girl.

DICK: Okay, so maybe you're not too old for MILFs.

TOM: I don't think you're getting what I mean.

DICK: *(beat)* Oh, okay. I get it.

TOM: Yeah?

DICK: Yeah. She broke your heart.

TOM: Who?

DICK: Penny. She's the one that got away. You're still pining for Penny!

TOM: No, that's not it at all.

DICK: It's okay man. It's okay. I understand. We've all been there. We've all got stories about the one that ripped our heart out and left it out on the curb of life to be stomped upon. That's why you and me - we do what we do. No emotion. No connection. Just the act. The Beast with Two Backs. The Bump and Grind. The Boom Boom Pow. The-

TOM: Alright. That's enough.

DICK: Trust me, man. Give yourself a chance to get'cha game back on. It's like riding a bike. You just need to get back in the saddle.

TOM: *(beat)* You're an idiot. *(Harriet enters the bar. She's looking around for someone.)*

DICK: That may be, but you will be thanking me later. I've got someone I want you to meet. *(Dick waves Harriet over.)* Tom, meet Harriet.

TOM: Hi.

HARRIET: Hi. Nice to meet you.

TOM: Nice to meet you, too.

HARRIET: Sorry I'm late. Took forever to find parking. *(Harriet sits down with them.)*

DICK: Yeah, that's NoHo for you.

TOM: Seriously.

HARRIET: So, Tom, what do you do?

TOM: I'm... uh, I'm a writer.

HARRIET: Really? Like, what do you write?

TOM: Well, screenplays mostly.

HARRIET: Anything I might have seen?

TOM: Not really. Unless you like movies of the week on SyFy.

HARRIET: Oh, I LOVE those!

TOM: Really?

HARRIET: Yeah! Did you write the one with the giant squid?

TOM: Yeah!

HARRIET: I love that one!

TOM: You're joking.

HARRIET: I'm serious! Greatest movie line ever: *(Quoting the movie in "badass action hero" voice)* "Who wants calamari?"

TOM: Yeah...

HARRIET: So, you wrote that?

TOM: Well, it was sort of a group effort. I had hel-

DICK: My boy's too humble. He's a genius. A regular Jack Nicklaus.

TOM: You mean Nicholson, and he's an actor.

DICK: Whatever. Point is, Tom hates taking credit where credit's due.

HARRIET: I see. Well, I think your writing is great.

TOM: ...Thanks.

DICK: Yeah, so Harriet and I met doing background work last week. She's new in town, and since I'm booked on that movie for the next few days, I was thinking you could show her around town.

TOM: What?

DICK: Sure dude.

TOM: No, I can't. I've got a lot of important stuff I do during the day.

HARRIET: It's okay, I don't want to b-

DICK: Dude, you're a freelance writer. Quit trying to act like you've got a real job.

TOM: I take my work very seriously.

DICK: Yeah. Writing about giant squids. C'mon, dude.

HARRIET: It's okay. I don't want you to feel obligated.

TOM: It's not that I feel obligated. Not at all. I just don't really know anyplace all that interesting.

HARRIET: Oh, I'm sure we could find... something... to do. *(Beat. Then, to Dick)* Can you order me a Double Vodka Tonic, easy on the Tonic?

DICK: Sure. *(Harriet goes to the ladies room.)*

TOM: What the HELL was that?

DICK: That's the sound of you gettin' back on that zebra's ass and gettin' some.

TOM: Okay, stop it with the zebra. She's gonna get plastered! How's she going to drive home?

DICK: I don't think she's planning on driving.

TOM: Well, someone's gotta give her a ride.

DICK: Don't look at me. I took the Metro.

TOM: *(beat)* You set me up. You totally set this up, didn't you.

DICK: What? Me? No. No. Never. *(Beat.)* Okay, okay. Yes. Yes, I did. I totally set this up.

TOM: Oh for God's sake.

DICK: I did this for you, bro. It's all for you. I've seen how down you've been and I just wanted to help you get-

TOM: *(interjecting)* -back on the zebra. I got it. You're a dick.

DICK: Yes. Yes, I am. It's short for Richard. The name. Not my penis.

TOM: What am I going to do?

DICK: Isn't it obvious? Give her a ride. Then take her home. She's totally jonesin' for your jock, dude.

TOM: I can't do this.

DICK: Yes. Yes you can. Here. Let me help lube up this evening's proceedings.

TOM: What? *(Dick waves to the waiter.)*

DICK: Garçon! Liquid Courage for my friend here and a double Vodka Tonic, easy on the Tonic for his latest conquest.

TOM: Will you stop it?

DICK: No. Not until you've planted your flag between her twin peaks. *(A Waiter enters carrying a tray with two glasses on it. One is full of a red liquid. He puts the red drink in front of Tom.)*

WAITER: Here you go. Double Vodka sans Tonic for the lady. Liquid Courage for the smooth operator.

DICK: Thanks, bro.

WAITER: No problem. Careful with the Liquid Courage, though. Strong stuff. *(The Waiter exits. Tom takes the drink and sniffs it.)*

TOM: Woof.

DICK: What?

TOM: Smells like paint thinner.

DICK: Well, it looks good. Just shoot it.

TOM: No.

DICK: C'mon.

TOM: Dude, hell no.

DICK: You can't let that go to waste.

TOM: Fine, you drink it.

DICK: What the hell. I'm not driving. *(Tom passes the drink to Dick, who shoots it back. Dick looks at Tom and is immediately smitten.)* Wow.

TOM: Strong stuff?

DICK: Yeah. Y'know, what say you and me bail?

TOM: Huh?

DICK: Let's go.

TOM: Why?

DICK: I'm bored.

TOM: But Harriet's-

DICK: Forget her, dude.

TOM: Why? *(Harriet reenters.)*

DICK: Ah, crap.

HARRIET: Sorry about that. There was a line.

TOM: It's okay.

DICK: Yeah, y'know, we were just about to go.

HARRIET: Oh?

TOM: No we weren't. It's okay.

DICK: Yes. We were.

HARRIET: Something wrong?

TOM: *(glaring at Dick)* No. No, everything's fine. So, Harriet. What do you do?

HARRIET: Well, I just moved here from Kansas. I'm doing background work, but I've already got a meeting with an agent and I just signed up for this awesome acting class.

DICK: *(interrupting)* Wow that's so fascinating.

TOM: Dick.

HARRIET: It's okay. Y'know Tom, maybe you and I should go?

DICK: No!

TOM: Maybe that's not a bad idea.

DICK: It is.

TOM: Why?

HARRIET: It's okay, we can stay if you want.

DICK: *(to Harriet)* You don't need to stay.

TOM: *Dick.* *(to Harriet)* Y'know, I'll have one more round.

HARRIET: Well, that's good. I hate to drink alone.

DICK: *(taking her drink and dumping it out over his shoulder)* Y'know, you shouldn't be drinking in your condition.

HARRIET & TOM: What?

DICK: What with the baby and all.

TOM: Baby?

HARRIET: What are you talking about? What the hell's going on here?

DICK: It's okay, hon. We won't be needing your services after all. *(Dick takes out his wallet and starts to remove some bills Then, to Tom.)* Seriously, man. She's just lookin' for a baby daddy. You shouldn't get involved with her. *(to Harriet)* This should cove-

TOM: Dude! What the hell are you doing?

DICK: It's okay, babe. I got this.

TOM: *(to Harriet)* I'm so sorry. I don't know what's gotten in to him.

DICK: Liquid Courage.

TOM: Shut up.

HARRIET: Whatever. I don't have to take this. *(Harriet glares at Dick. After a beat, she holds her hand out, expectantly. Beat. Dick hands Harriet a wad of money. She thumbs through it.)* You are so not paying me enough for this crap.

DICK: Yeah, yeah, yeah. Go. *(Harriet exits. A long pause.)*

TOM: What the hell was that?

DICK: What?

TOM: You paid her to come here and meet me?

DICK: No, I paid her to come here and then go home and have sex with you.

TOM: You what?

DICK: And then I changed my mind.

TOM: WHY?

DICK: Trust me, it's for the best. She had Herpes anyway.

TOM: WHAT?

DICK: Dude, calm down.

TOM: You set me up on a blind date with a hooker? A pregnant hooker? With Herpes? Then you send her aw- What?

DICK: It's okay. She's not really pregnant. I just made that up. Not sure about the herpes thing, though.

TOM: WHAT HAS GOTTEN IN TO YOU?

DICK: Liquid Courage. *(Tom stands angrily and leans over the table at Dick.)*

TOM: What does that have to do with any-

DICK: It's given me the balls to finally do this. *(Dick stands up, grabs Tom's face and kisses him full on the lips. Tom is shocked and pulls away. Beat. Tom kisses Dick back. Break.)*

TOM: ...How did you know?

DICK: You're just a dog looking for a good bone.

TOM: I thought you said a zebra doesn't change its spots.

DICK: Yeah, well... tastes evolve, right?

TOM: Right. *(beat)* So, you need a ride?

DICK: Sure. Can you take me home afterward? *(Blackout.)*

Props

Assorted drinks and glassware (Tom, Dick, Harriet)

Serving Tray (Waiter)

WANNA BET?

Wanna Bet? premiered on April 3rd, 2010 as a part of Theatre Unleashed's 24-Hour Theatre Festival, *Acting Our Age: The Terrible Twos*. It featured David Shackelford as Tim, Courtney Bell as Sharon and Alexis Kupka as Dana. Directed by Ben Atkinson. Stage Manager Erin Scott.

WANNA BET?

Setting

Tim & Dana's Apartment. It's simple – the kind of place newlyweds would have if they put it together on a shoestring budget. Couch, coffee table with remote control on it, end table, small dining table (which a bag of Chinese food sits on top of, still warm) for two – all crammed into one room. Idealistic romantics would call a home like this "intimate."

Cast

TIM – *Dana's husband, late 20's - early 30's. Competitive. Not a fan of his wife's best friend.*

DANA – *Tim's wife and Sharon's best friend, late 20's – early 30's. Birthday girl caught in the middle.*

SHARON – *Dana's best friend, late 20's – early 30's. Competitive. Not a fan of her best friend's husband.*

Scene

Tim enters, carrying a small shopping bag and a pizza in a "to go" box. He notices the apartment is clean for the first time since they moved in.

TIM: Awww man! I hope she didn't feel she had to do this. It's her birthday! She shouldn't have cleaned. *(Tim sets the pizza box down on the coffee table. He turns and notices the Chinese food.)* Chinese? *(calling out)* Dana? *(beat)* Baby? You home? *(weakly)* Surpriiiise. *(Tim glances into the bedroom doorway. Seeing no one, he returns to the Chinese food. He notices a DVD next to the food. Distastefully:)* Twilight? Really? Aww… poor thing. Well, I guess we won't be needing this tonight. *(Tim picks up the Chinese food and DVD and starts looking for a place to put them. The latch on the door starts to turn. Tim dives behind the couch. Sharon, Dana's best friend, enters with a small birthday cake.*

Tim jumps up from behind the couch.) Surprise! *(Sharon jumps back, startled. Tim, realizing who it is, also jumps back.)*

SHARON: TIM!

TIM: Sharon!

BOTH: What are you doing here?

TIM: You go first.

SHARON: I'm spending Dana's birthday with her. She called me last week and told me she wanted to hang out tonight. What are you doing back? I thought you were supposed to be up in San Francisco on business.

TIM: There was no trip. I lied so I could surprise Dana. You scared the crap out of me. How you get in here?

SHARON: Dana gave me the spare when you first moved in.

TIM: Oh…

SHARON: *(beat)* She didn't tell you?

TIM: No.

SHARON: Well, if you're wondering where it went…

TIM: Yeah. Thanks. I see that. Good to know.

SHARON: You're welcome, by the way.

TIM: For what?

SHARON: *(indicating the room)* All this.

TIM: YOU cleaned?

SHARON: Me? Oh hell no. I hired a maid.

TIM: Well, thank you.

SHARON: No problem. *(under her breath)* Somebody had to.

TIM: So, what did you have planned for tonight?

SHARON: Girl's night in. You keep hogging her all the time now, so I've got to do something.

TIM: Well, we are married, y'know.

SHARON: *(playfully)* I know! How dare you?

TIM: I'm such a bastard.

SHARON: You really are.

TIM: Girl's night in, huh?

SHARON: Yeah, her favorite food, her favorite cake, favorite movie… even if it's not as good as the book…

TIM: You got her General Fung's. That's not her favorite food.

SHARON: Yes it is.

TIM: No, it's not. Her favorite food is the thick-crust pizza from Little Tony's. *(indicating the pizza box on the coffee table)* She loves the burnt pepperoni pieces the best.

SHARON: No, that's your favorite food.

TIM: Well, it's OUR favorite food. It's grown on her. We barely go to General Fung's any more.

SHARON: You two "barely" go there, sure. We meet there for lunch once a week. What kind of cake did you get her?

TIM: Marble with Cinnamon Hazlenut filling. You?

SHARON: Tiramisu cake.

TIM: Gift?

SHARON: I renewed her annual pass to Disneyland.

TIM: VIP Parking?

SHARON: Of course.

TIM: Ooh… you're good. But not good enough beat what I got her.

SHARON: Wanna bet?

TIM: Sure.

SHARON: Okay, wha'd you get her?

TIM: It's a surprise.

SHARON: She hates surprises.

TIM: She won't hate this one.

SHARON: In my ten years of knowing her, she's never – EVER – liked a surprise of any kind.

TIM: *(doing his best Adam Savage impersonation)* Well, I reject your reality and substitute my own.

SHARON: Huh?

TIM: *Mythbusters*? Y'know… those two guys that blow stuff up on Discovery Channel?

SHARON: *(indicating herself)* Head cheerleader.

TIM: It's on a freakin' tee shirt!

SHARON: Whatever! Wha'd you get her?

TIM: Can't tell you. It'll ruin the surprise.

SHARON: You can't do that.

TIM: Says who?

SHARON: No bet, then.

TIM: Fine. You couldn't beat it anyway.

SHARON: You're on!

TIM: Terms?

SHARON: I win, we hang out and all watch *Twilight*.

TIM: Not on my TV you won't.

SHARON: Scared you'll lose?

TIM: No.

SHARON: What are you worried about, then?

TIM: Touché. Alright, if I win, we all watch *Fellowship of the Ring.*

SHARON: Fine by me. That elf is easy on the eyes.

TIM: Liv Tyler?

SHARON: Legolas.

TIM: HA! Head cheerleader, my ass.

SHARON: Shut up! He's pretty! *(A frazzled and exhausted Dana enters through the front door.)*

DANA: Shar? You here? Who you talking to? *(Dana clears the doorway and sees both Tim and Sharon.)*

TIM: Surprise!

DANA: Hi! Ohmigod! What are you doing home?

TIM: Hi, baby. *(Tim and Dana embrace and kiss, quickly, then Dana turns her attention to Sharon.)*

DANA: Hey, stranger!

SHARON: Hey Dana! Happy Birthday! *(The girls embrace.)*

DANA: Thanks!

SHARON: I brought you dinner from General Fung's. Beef & Broccoli and some Veggie Stir Fry.

DANA: Oh... thank you.

SHARON: Is that alright?

DANA: Yeah, it's just…

TIM: Well, I got you your favorite.

DANA: My favorite?

TIM: Pepperoni pizza from Little Toni's.

DANA: Oh! Thank you. That's great, babe… really great. Yeah. Uh, do you mind if we save that?

TIM: Huh?

DANA: It's so greasy.

TIM: But it's your favorite! You should have your favorite on your birthday.

SHARON: Here! Have some steamed veggies. No grease on them.

DANA: *(beat, resigned)* Alright. *(Sharon taunts Tim behind Dana's back.)*

TIM: Well, when you're done with that, we've got something really special for you.

DANA: Oh, guys, it's okay, I'm really no- *(Tim and Sharon proudly display their cakes and speak simultaneously:)*

TIM: Cinnamon Hazlenut Cake!

SHARON: Tiramisu Cake!

DANA: What?

SHARON: Well, you've got a choice. Marble cake with Cinnamon Hazlenut or… Tiramisu!

TIM: Not just any Cinnamon Hazlenut cake, babe. It's from Mike's Pastry, just like the cake from our rehearsal dinner.

SHARON: Well, I made the Tiramisu cake myself. *(Dana blanches a little at the thought of Sharon's baking.)*

TIM: So, which would you prefer, sweetheart?

DANA: I'm not really feelin' like cake ton-

SHARON: It's your birthday! You can't skip cake on your birthday! That's against the rules or something! C'mon, pick one!

DANA: Okay! Fine! I'll have a piece of the Cinnamon Hazlenut. But just a small one. I'm not really in the mood fo- *(she catches Tim silently taunting Sharon)* What are you doing?

TIM: Huh?

DANA: What are you two doing?

TIM & SHARON: Nothing.

DANA: Bullshit. What's going on? *(Tim and Sharon look at each other, guiltily.)* Oh, I don't believe this. You guys made a bet, didn't you? Didn't you? *(They sheepishly nod the affirmative.)* Why does this always happen with you two? EVERY TIME! You bet on my birthday. ON MY FREAKIN' BIRTHDAY! What the he- *(she stops to gather herself)* Y'know what, guys? Thank you both, but I've already had a really, really shitty day, and this just topped it off. My boss yelled at me for being twenty minutes late because I couldn't find any parking. All of my kids were monsters. I had the Hell Twins for two hours and they fought the entire time, followed by Pablo and then Skylar, who decided he'd rather lay on the floor than do his math homework. Some jackass at Coffee Bean spilled his drink all over me during my lunch and totally tried to feel me up claiming he wanted to "help clean me off," my feet hurt, I was stuck on the 405 for two hours trying to get home and to top it all off, I feel like I'm coming down with the flu. Again. Frankly, I'm not in the mood for a party this evening. And I sure as hell am not going to have one if it means you two are trying to prove who knows me better. I HATE that! Neither of you asked me how I'm doing or what I really wanted tonight, by the way. Thanks for that. So, I don't care what y'all do, but this is stupid. I'm going to go to go throw up and go to bed.

TIM: Baby, is there anything I can do for y-

DANA: Oh, it's too late for that, bucko. Your ass is on the couch tonight. *(she turns to leave, but then turns back)* Oh, Shar, thanks for getting the place straightened up. Can you leave the card of the service you hired before you go? I like what they did.

SHARON: How'd you know?

DANA: Please, like he'd ever clean and like you'd ever do it yourself. I know you both too well. Happy freakin' Birthday. *(Dana exits into the bedroom.)*

TIM: Wow.

SHARON: Yeah. *(beat)* How are we going to settle this now?

TIM: Seriously. Well, the way I see it, we're one and one.

SHARON: Agreed. We never did get to the presents.

TIM: Nope.

SHARON: So, what did you get her? *(Tim glances at the bedroom door, leans over and whispers something in Sharon's ear. She's blown away. Defeated, she picks up* Lord of the Rings *from off the table and hands it to Tim. He puts it in the DVD player. Sharon goes and grabs her birthday cake and two forks. Tim starts the movie. Sharon hands him a fork. They sit on the couch together and begin digging in to the cake from right off the platter.)*

TIM: Good call on the Tiramisu.

SHARON: Thanks! *(beat)* If Dana were here, she'd totally want to watch *Twilight*.

TIM: Wanna bet? *(Blackout.)*

Props

Twilight DVD (Tim)

Fellowship of the Ring DVD (Tim)

DVD Remote (Sharon)

DVD Player (Sharon)

Bag of Chinese Food (Sharon)

Pizza Box (Tim)

2 Cakes (Tim, Sharon)

CUT BY OCCAM'S RAZOR

Cut By Occam's Razor premiered on June 19th, 2010 as a part of Theatre Unleashed's summer 24-Hour Theatre Festival, *Boarding the Mothership*. It featured Jude Evans as the Tall One and Ana Therese Lopez as the Short One. Directed by Dennis Gerstin. Stage Manager Erin Scott.

CUT BY OCCAM'S RAZOR

<u>Setting</u>

Nighttime in the Nevada Desert, 1946.

<u>Cast</u>

TALL ONE – *A tall alien.*

SHORT ONE – *A short alien.*

<u>Scene</u>

The two aliens are standing over the crashed remains of their ship.

TALL ONE: No, seriously. Just paint a couple of Swastikas on the body. No one will know.

SHORT ONE: *(beat)* Huh?

TALL ONE: Y'know. Swastikas. The Sun Cross. Thor's Hammer.

SHORT ONE: What are you talking about?

TALL ONE: It's the symbol of the Third Reich. Hitler's Germany. It'll be perfect.

SHORT ONE: Dumbass. We crashed our fucking ship in the middle of the NEVADA Desert and now you want to paint the wreckage up so it looks like we belong to a group of genocidal maniacs?

TALL ONE: ...Yes.

SHORT ONE: What is wrong with you?

TALL ONE: I'm just trying to blend in.

SHORT ONE: We're in the middle of the United States of AMERICA! Land of the Free! Home of the Brave! Baseball, mom and apple pie! They just WON the war and you want to make us look like we're from the OTHER SIDE??

TALL ONE: Trust me.

SHORT ONE: Trust you. Right. That's what you said when you told me we didn't need the running lights and you'd be just fine flying in the dark.

TALL ONE: I told you we couldn't risk being seen.

SHORT ONE: More like you couldn't risk seeing where you were going.

TALL ONE: Har har.

SHORT ONE: I still don't get where the Swastikas come in.

TALL ONE: It's simple.

SHORT ONE: Nothing is EVER simple with you.

TALL ONE: This is.

SHORT ONE: Bullshit.

TALL ONE: I'll prove it.

SHORT ONE: You do that.

TALL ONE: I will.

SHORT ONE: Okay.

TALL ONE: Okay.

SHORT ONE: Start talkin'.

TALL ONE: I am!

SHORT ONE: No, you're stalling.

TALL ONE: No I'm not!

SHORT ONE: Yes you a- Get on with it!

TALL ONE: Alright! *(beat)* Jeez...

SHORT ONE: C'mon Himmler. We're wasting precious cycles.

TALL ONE: How's your German accent?

SHORT ONE: Shitty. Yours?

TALL ONE: *(affecting a bad German accent)* Ist gut.

SHORT ONE: No, *ist* not.

TALL ONE: We'll be fine. We're going to need to go under cover. You'll be the crazy American test pilot and I'll be the mad German scientist.

SHORT ONE: What's that going to do for us?

TALL ONE: Simple. When the US Army comes to investigate, we tell them we're with a Top Secret Project, that the wreckage is from some super-secret Nazi aircraft I built in The Fatherland which you captured and brought back. We get 'em to haul it to an airbase somewhere and help us rebuild it. Then, once it's all back together, you and I climb on board for a "test flight" and soar back home!

SHORT ONE: Just like that.

TALL ONE: Just like that.

SHORT ONE: It'll never work.

TALL ONE: Why not?

SHORT ONE: Because.

TALL ONE: Because why?

SHORT ONE: Because we lost our nav computer, our hull is cracked, and where on Earth are we going to find a Tritanium Positron Recycler? Do you have ANY idea how primitive human technology is? It will be at least a millennium before they've even got a cheap-ass generic analog!

TALL ONE: You got a better idea?

SHORT ONE: No.

TALL ONE: Then we go with my plan.

SHORT ONE: I hate your plan.

TALL ONE: Then give me an alternative!

SHORT ONE: *(beat)* Why not just tell them?

TALL ONE: Tell them what?

SHORT ONE: What we really are.

TALL ONE: You're not serious.

SHORT ONE: I am.

TALL ONE: We can't.

SHORT ONE: Sure we can. We can greet them with open arms. Reveal our true nature to them in an overture of peace. Offer them our extensive understanding of the galaxy in exchange for a welcome place in their society. With our superior intellect and knowledge of advanced technology, we could help them! Advanced farming techniques. New medicines. Alternative energy development. The greatest generation of humanity to date just saved this world from the brink of utter destruction. They're ushering in an era of peace the likes of which they've never known before! Together we can make this world a better place. Now is the perfect time to introduce them to the larger universe. We'd be like gods among them. Maybe they'll even let us take mates.

TALL ONE: Won't happen.

SHORT ONE: Why not?

TALL ONE: *(incredulous)* Why not?

SHORT ONE: Yeah. Why not?

TALL ONE: Fear. That's why. If we tell them we're not from this planet, they'll kill us. They'll shoot us, gun us down like animals. They'll mutilate our remains. Cut us apart and harvest our organs to see what makes us tick. Or worse. They'll lock us away in some isolated room with white padded walls where men in long white coats and thin black ties and black horn rimmed glasses and pocket protectors will stare at us through inch-thick bulletproof windows all day and all night and make little notes on clipboards about everything we do. Every time you blink, every time you cough, every time you fart, they'll make a fucking note about it. But they'll never listen to us. They'll never try to really communicate with us. They'll never, ever try to treat us even remotely like equals even though we are the far superior species. We'll be like zoo pets. Lab animals to them. If there is one thing our mission of anthropological observation has taught me is that humans fear what they cannot understand, and they do not tolerate what they fear. They can't even get past the diversity in their physical appearances to accept one another. I'm pretty sure that means that beings of our nature would be like the distant intergalactic uncle that no one likes to talk about ever since we got hammered and pissed all over ourselves at the family Thanksgiving ten years ago. We're safer crammed into these skin suits like German sausage. And that is why they don't deserve us.

SHORT ONE: If you think that's the case, we should avoid them altogether.

TALL ONE: No!

SHORT ONE: Yes! You just said so yourself. If they discover our true nature, we're calamari. Or, worse yet, stuck living in a Petri dish for the rest of our lives. We should gather the remains of the ship, find a cave somewhere and hole up for however long it takes for us to get the interstellar transmitter and receiver working again and call for help.

TALL ONE: Absolutely not.

SHORT ONE: Why?

TALL ONE: If I'm going to be stuck on this rock for generations while we work on finding a way home, I don't want to be alone.

SHORT ONE: Okay...

TALL ONE: Besides, we don't have time. That was a U.S. Army outpost we flew over a few miles back. There's no way they missed our crash. I'm sure they're on their way here now.

SHORT ONE: Well. That certainly settles things.

TALL ONE: Exactly. Now help me find something we can use to decorate the remains.

SHORT ONE: Okay... but you still haven't explained why Swastikas.

TALL ONE: Occam's razor.

SHORT ONE: Huh?

TALL ONE: The simplest explanation is usually the correct one. We present them with the simplest explanation for our presence and the presence of a destroyed space- er, AIRcraft and most likely they'll accept it, no questions asked.

SHORT ONE: You actually think your plan is simple?

TALL ONE: I didn't say "simple." I said "simplest." If they think Hitler had advanced technology, the Americans will do everything they can to tear it apart, figure it out and adapt it to their own purposes. We'll use that ambition to help get us off this godforsaken rock much quicker than we could on our own.

SHORT ONE: If you say so.

TALL ONE: I do say so.

SHORT ONE: Y'know, someone's bound to talk.

TALL ONE: Hmm?

SHORT ONE: We didn't just fly over a single Army outpost. You seem to forget we had a nice joyride around most of Middle America this evening. People must have seen us. Word will get out that this is a spacecraft. Suspicions will grow.

TALL ONE: Please. They wouldn't even know what to make of us. We looked like some sort of... unidentified...flying... whirligig to them. Which is why we can get away with this story. We don't need to give an explanation that everyone believes. Just the majority. The rest will be dismissed as nuts and lunatics.

SHORT ONE: Maybe we can have the Army say it was a weather balloon that crashed or something.

TALL ONE: Now you've got it! *(They hear trucks approaching.)*

SHORT ONE: Hey, I just thought of something.

TALL ONE: Look! Here come the boys in olive green now!

SHORT ONE: I just thought of something.

TALL ONE: What?

SHORT ONE: You said we're a part of some government thing, right?

TALL ONE: Yeah?

SHORT ONE: What's it called?

TALL ONE: What's what called?

SHORT ONE: The operation.

TALL ONE: Huh?

SHORT ONE: This top secret operation that smuggled a German scientist and a prototype Nazi aircraft to a remote desert testing facility for American analysis.

TALL ONE: I don't know.

SHORT ONE: You don't know?

TALL ONE: *(beat)* What's in your pockets?

SHORT ONE: What the hell do you mean you don't-

TALL ONE: Just answer my damn question.

SHORT ONE: Some gum, set of keys, a paperclip, some belly button lin-

TALL ONE: Paperclip. Operation Paperclip.

SHORT ONE: Seriously?

TALL ONE: Sure. It'll work.

SHORT ONE: I hope you're right about this.

TALL ONE: Don't worry. It'll be fine. Trust me. *(to the soldiers off stage, with bad German accent)* Friends! Over here! Ich bin ein Berliner! *(The Tall One exits towards the soldiers with hands raised in welcome.)*

SHORT ONE: We are SO fucked. *(Blackout.)*

<u>Props</u>

Assorted Spacecraft Parts (Tall One)

YELLOW MEANS CAUTION

Yellow Means Caution premiered on February 5th, 2011 as a part of Theatre Unleashed's 24-Hour Theatre Festival, *Can't Buy Me Love*. It was inspired by The Beatles' *Yellow Submarine*. The World Premiere featured Derek Houck as Max and Jenn Scuderi as Loretta. Directed and Stage Managed by Erin Scott.

YELLOW MEANS CAUTION

Setting

Inside Max and Loretta's apartment. Present day.

Cast

MAX – *Uptight, hooked on video games. 20's-30's.*

LORETTA – *Max's wife. Neglected, frustrated. 20's-30's.*

Scene

Loretta has just finished painting the interior of their home a garish yellow. She's looking around at her handiwork, paintbrush in hand. She's determined to like it. Max enters.

MAX: Hi bab- Whoa!
LORETTA: Do you like it?
MAX: The paint?
LORETTA: Yeah.
MAX: It's very…
LORETTA: Yeah?
MAX: Verrrry…
LORETTA: Yeah?
MAX: Yellow, hon. It's very, very yellow. Like, holy crap it's Yellow.
LORETTA: Yes.
MAX: Like Big Bird just exploded in here Ye-
LORETTA: You hate it.
MAX: No! No, I don't. Not at all. It's just… wow. Y'know… bright.
LORETTA: So you hate it.
MAX: No. No. Not at all. *(half a beat)* Yes. Yes, I hate it. What in God's name possessed you to paint our apartment canary yellow?
LORETTA: Because it's… nice!

MAX: It's day-glo! It's brighter than the Vegas strip in here right now and the lights aren't even on!

LORETTA: Max, it's not that bad.

MAX: Hon. It is.

LORETTA: Well, I thought we just needed to let a little sunshine in here.

MAX: Open the blinds, then.

LORETTA: None of them get good directional light, and it was just so dreary in here I just had to do something. So I went down to the Home Depot and I bought a few gallons of this. *(holds up a paint chip)* Yellow Submarine. It's a very happy color based on a very happy song.

MAX: Seriously?

LORETTA: It was even on sale. Two gallons for the price of one.

MAX: I'm sure it was. Can we change it?

LORETTA: Why?

MAX: Because it's YELLOW.

LORETTA: I like it. I like our apartment-

MAX: Neon Highlighter Nuclear Yellow-Cake Uranium Yellow.

LORETTA: Yes. And it's staying this way. *(Max takes a moment to consider his options. Is it really worth a fight right now?)*

MAX: Well, maybe it'll dry darker.

LORETTA: Oh, I doubt it.

MAX: Not helping. *(beat)* Well, let me know when it dries. I'll help get all the pictures back on the wall. *(muttering to himself)* Maybe that will cut down on the glare. *(Max starts to head toward their bedroom.)* I'm going to get changed. What say we go out to eat tonight? *(Loretta stands in the center of the living room, awaiting Max's reaction. Max, offstage:)* OH MY GOD. *(Loretta cringes. Max comes running back in to the living room.)* YOU PAINTED THE BEDROOM YELLOW TOO?!?

LORETTA: And the bathroom.

MAX: Wha...? The bath- *(He glances into the bathroom. Beat.)* You painted the toilet. We have a Yellow Submarine-colored toilet. I didn't even know porcelain would take paint.

LORETTA: Neither did I! But it totally does!

MAX: What else did you paint?

LORETTA: Well… the kitchen… the closets… the pantry… the laundry nook…

MAX: Basically every flat surface in the apartment. How much did you buy?

LORETTA: It was all on sale. Two-for-one.

MAX: Honey. What's wrong?

LORETTA: What?

MAX: What's gotten in to you?

LORETTA: Nothing!

MAX: Then why paint everything? Normal, rational people don't do that.

LORETTA: It was on sale. The paint was on sale.

MAX: Okay, fine. I understand that. But why THIS color? And why ALL this color? Surely they must have had other colors available? *(Loretta takes a long pause.)*

LORETTA: Well… I wanted our home to be a happy color. Y'know. So we could have a little happiness back in here. I just thought that…

MAX: Wait, wait, wait… whoa… are you unhappy? Is that it?

LORETTA: *(beat)* No. Everything's fine.

MAX: C'mon baby.

LORETTA: Everything's. Fine.

MAX: You know you can tell me if something's wrong.

LORETTA: Oh, can I?

MAX: Yes. You can.

LORETTA: Well, good. Everything's fine right now, but I'll tell you when something's wrong. Okay? Right now I just wanted to let some sunshine in. Simple as that.

MAX: *(beat)* Fine. *(beat)* Where's my controller? If you're not going to talk to me about this now, then I'm going to take a break and blow off some steam.

LORETTA: Here. *(Loretta hands Max his game system controller. It's been painted yellow, too. Beat. Max looks at it with disgust, then glares at her with barely-contained frustration as he takes it and hits the "on" button for the game system. He turns to the TV [set towards the house] and starts thumbing through the menus. After a moment, he realizes something's wrong.)*

MAX: What th… What happened to my profile? Where are my saved games?

LORETTA: Hmm?

MAX: What happened to my games? What did you do??

LORETTA: I don't know. Something about a factory reset. Honestly, I was lucky to figure out how to turn the thing on.

MAX: Factory rese- What?!? What the FUCK, Loretta? WHAT the FUCK?!? WHAT THE FUCK!!!

LORETTA: It's all gone. And your little discs, too. *(Max frantically opens some game cases. She's painted all the bottoms of the discs yellow. He holds one up and displays it for all to see.)* Funny thing about those discs. You need to use this stuff called Plasti-Dip to get it to stick. Costs a little extra, but I even managed to find it in the Happy Color.

MAX: You've ruined them. All of my games. My system. Why? Why would you do that? That's my life's work! I've lost everything!

LORETTA: Everything? You've lost everything?

MAX: Yes! Do you know how long I spent beating those games, unlocking those trophies, earning those achievements?!?

LORETTA: Years!

MAX: Yes! Years! Years and years! And it's all gone!

LORETTA: Yes it is.

MAX: How am I going to get that back?

LORETTA: Better question is, how am I?

MAX: What?

LORETTA: You spent years in front of that game system every night after coming home from work and I spent years cooking, and cleaning and doing your laundry and falling asleep alone and unsatisfied in our bed EVERY NIGHT while you played your stupid games until the crack of fucking dawn. I'm a widow. I'm alone and I'm locked up in this little shoebox apartment prison with you because you ignore me and I just couldn't take it anymore. Y'know, I almost wish it was another woman you were paying all that attention to because then I'd know that at least your joystick still worked. But you've pissed away years of our marriage in front of that goddamn TV playing with yourself, and that's time that's supposed to be ours. How am I going to get that time back? *(Loretta's ready to cry. Max is at a loss. It's a lot for him to handle all at once.)*

MAX: But… destroying my system? You could have tr-

LORETTA: I did! I did try!

MAX: How?

LORETTA: How? How?!? Where do I begin? What about your birthday this year? You were so excited to get your new, stupid fucking *Call of Duty: Secret Quest-*

MAX: *Black Ops.*

LORETTA: *Black Ops*! Whatever! That you completely blew off the dinner I made for the two of us. I made your favorite and I even had a special desert for you.

MAX: Really? I didn't see anything in the kitchen except some Reddi-Whip… *(She shoots him a glare. Beat)* Oh…

LORETTA: Yeah, you were up all night long playing that damn game. I was up all night long alone in our bedroom, crying. I could go on.

MAX: Baby…

LORETTA: What?

MAX: I'm sorry… but that's still no excuse for what you did.

LORETTA: What?!

MAX: You destroyed my stuff!

LORETTA: Are you serious?

MAX: Yes! Yes I am. Where the hell do you get off doing that? I mean, I understand that you're upset – and you're right to be – but this…

LORETTA: What was I supposed to do?!

MAX: You could have talked to me!

LORETTA: I can't!

MAX: So instead of trying, you just bottle everything up until you're compelled to paint everything in our home piss yellow in a passive-aggressive fit?

LORETTA: Passive-aggressive?

MAX: What the hell else would you call it?

LORETTA: I don't know how to talk to you anymore, you know that? It took me doing something like this- *(indicating the painted controller)* -to get you to pay attention to me at all! *(beat)* Sometimes I feel like I don't even know you anymore.

MAX: What?

LORETTA: Ever since we got married, it seems like you've completely changed. All you do is go to work, come home and play games by yourself. You used to play with me. And I don't just mean in bed. We used to enjoy spending time together doing all kinds of stuff. But now, I don't even know what we've got in common anymore. *(Loretta stares at Max, who is considering everything that's been said.)*

MAX: So… what do we do then?

LORETTA: I don't know.

MAX: *(beat)* Do you… do you think it would be worth trying?

LORETTA: Trying what? To make things work between us?

MAX: Yeah.

LORETTA: I don't even know where to begin.

MAX: *(beat)* Do you want to try counseling?

LORETTA: Why?

MAX: Because… I want to try something. Anything.

LORETTA: What's the point? I don't even know you anymore and you think I'm a passive-aggressive bitch.

MAX: *(he indicates the game discs)* Well...

LORETTA: Not helping.

MAX: *(beat)* How about because I love you?

LORETTA: Please.

MAX: I do.

LORETTA: It's going to take a lot more than just saying it to get me to believe that.

MAX: Okay.

LORETTA: Okay? Okay what? As in "Okay, I'll do it" or "Okay, I give up?"

MAX: Okay as in… Okay. Let's try to fix this and see what happens.

LORETTA: If that's what you want…

MAX: It is.

LORETTA: Okay.

MAX: Okay. *(beat)* I'm sorry. *(Loretta looks at him as if to say "seriously?")* I know it's going to take a lot more than that to fix this, but I thought that would be a good place to start. I'm sorry. I feel horrible, Loretta. I'm so sorry I neglected you and made you feel this way. I'm sorry I forced you to resort to this to get through to me. I'm sorry I wasn't there for you.

LORETTA: *(beat)* Thank you. *(They both sit on the couch together, awkwardly. It's clear that it's going to take a lot of work to mend their relationship but at least they're making a start.)*

MAX: *(looking around)* I hate this color.

LORETTA: *(beat)* So do I.

MAX: Yeah?

LORETTA: Yeah. I really, really hate this color. *(They look at each other. Their expressions are strained, stressed... but they still manage slight smiles at one another. Somewhere inside each of them we see a flicker of hope. **Blackout.**)*

<u>Props</u>

Yellow Paint Chips (Loretta)

Assorted Paint Supplies (Loretta)

Painted Video Game Controller (Max)

Painted Video Game Discs and Cases (Max)

PAVED WITH GOOD INTENTIONS

Paved With Good Intentions premiered on March 26th, 2011 as a part of Theatre Unleashed's annual 24-Hour Theatre Festival and birthday celebration, *Acting Our Age: Thoroughly Three*. It featured Tim Harrington as Korbyn and Crafty St. James as Zamzar. Directed by Lee Pollero. Stage Manager Erin Scott.

PAVED WITH GOOD INTENTIONS

Setting

Inside Chad's apartment. Present day.

Cast

ZAMZAR – *Epic Level Thief & Master Assassin in game. Socially handicapped and awkward in real life. 20's-40's.*

KORBYN – *Casual gamer. Part time fighter in the guild. Has a life. 20's-30's.*

Scene

The scene opens inside the apartment of Chad, better known to his online friends as Strath Darkfellow, Epic Level Death Knight. His equally-über guild mate, Paul (aka - Zamzar the Rogue) sits on Strath's couch in a stained tee shirt, sweat pants and sneakers. A bulging backpack sits on the floor in front of him. He has a piece of cake on a plate in one hand and a fork in the other. The rest of the mostly-consumed sheet cake sits on the coffee table in front of him.

The apartment is sparse. A couch, table and chair. There's a half-assed attempt at birthday decorations – a single balloon, maybe some ratty streamers. It's implied that Strath's super-sweet gaming PC is hooked up in his "command center," formerly known as the spare bedroom down the hall. Zamzar looks like he's been waiting a while. There's a knock at the door. Zamzar excitedly gets up, brushes the crumbs off his chest and runs to answer it. At the door is Jason, also known as Korbyn the Warrior. He's a casual gamer – not nearly as hardcore as Strath or Zamzar. Unlike his other two guild mates, he actually has a life.

ZAMZAR: Strath, I presume?

KORBYN: No, I'm Korbyn. Actually, my real name is Jas-

ZAMZAR: *(cutting him off)* Ah! Our Level 35 Fighter. Well met, Korbyn!

KORBYN: Good to meet you, too. I take it you're…

ZAMZAR: Zamzar, Epic Level Thief and Master Assassin, at your service.

KORBYN: Zamzar. Right. Seen you in the guild chat room online. Nice to meet you IRL.

ZAMZAR: You too.

KORBYN: So, is this the party?

ZAMZAR: So far.

KORBYN: Who else is coming?

ZAMZAR: Well… You. Me. Strath…

KORBYN: Anyone else?

ZAMZAR: *(Thinks it over for a moment. Then-)* No.

KORBYN: Really? That kind of sucks.

ZAMZAR: Well, the rest of the Guild will be online for the raid later tonight. We'll get to par-tay with them then.

KORBYN: Why aren't they here in person?

ZAMZAR: Well, of course I'm here because I'm his most trusted Lieutenant. Consider it an honor to receive this invitation, Warrior Korbyn. Not just anyone gets invited to our Lord and Guild Master Strath Darkfellow's surprise in-person birthday party.

KORBYN: Wow… I had no idea. *(beat)* So, why'd you pick me? Was it because of my performance against the dragon we took down last week?

ZAMZAR: You're the only one that was local. Everyone else lives out of state and couldn't afford plane fare.

KORBYN: Oh.

ZAMZAR: Yes. *(An awkward silence.)*

KORBYN: My real name's Ja-

ZAMZAR: We have no need for "real names" here, Korbyn.

KORBYN: Right… *(Another awkward silence.)* So, where is the birthday boy?

ZAMZAR: Strath? I don't know.

KORBYN: What, did he get lost?

ZAMZAR: Coming back to his home? I doubt it.

KORBYN: Oh, so this is his place! Okay. Cool. So, do you guys live together?

ZAMZAR: No. I live on the West Side.

KORBYN: *(beat)* Does he know we're here?

ZAMZAR: Of course not!

KORBYN: Wait, what?

ZAMZAR: Uh, that would ruin the surprise?

KORBYN: So, how'd you get in?

ZAMZAR: I'm an Epic Level Thief and Master Assassin.

KORBYN: … in the game. *(Zamzar shrugs as if to say "tomato, tomahto.")* Okay, so where's Strath?

ZAMZAR: Probably still out looking for me.

KORBYN: Huh?

ZAMZAR: Well, I had to get him out of his command center somehow.

KORBYN: Command center?

ZAMZAR: Indeed! Our Dark Lord, the Death Knight Strath Darkfellow oversees the guild from his command center in the next room. It's quite impressive. He's got one of the sweetest gaming rigs I've ever seen. Four linked monitors, wireless controllers, liquid-cooled hexa-core processor and enough RAM to-

KORBYN: *(interjecting)* I see. Sounds like you know your way around it pretty well.

ZAMZAR: Who, me? No. I never even saw it in real life until today. He posted the specs online in the guild forum months ago. I've been saving up to buy one just like it myself for a while now.

KORBYN: Wow.

ZAMZAR: Do you like what I did with the place?

KORBYN: Huh?

ZAMZAR: The decorations for the party. Do you like them?

KORBYN: *(beat, looking around)* Sure…

ZAMZAR: I picked them out myself.

KORBYN: *(changing the subject)* So what's the plan for the party if it's just the three of us?

ZAMZAR: Well, I'm sure Strath will want to log back in right away after being gone for so long. I'm sure he'll have a lot he'll need to catch up on.

KORBYN: You mean we're just going to sit here and watch him play the game?

ZAMZAR: No! Of course not! *(beat)* He'll be in the command center. We can log in from out here. *(Zamzar produces his laptop from his bag.)*

KORBYN: Are you kidding me?

ZAMZAR: Don't worry. He's got Wi-Fi and a dedicated high speed line. Did you bring your system with you?

KORBYN: What? No!

ZAMZAR: Oh, it's okay. I brought my spare just in case. Here! Zamzar produces a second laptop from the same bag.

KORBYN: You're not serious.

ZAMZAR: … Yes.

KORBYN: That's ridiculous! I thought we were getting together to socialize. Hang out. Y'know… talk!

ZAMZAR: Of course! We'll do all that. *(beat)* In the game.

KORBYN: Dude, I drove all the way out from Pomona for this?

ZAMZAR: *(beat)* I got us a cake. *(Zamzar indicates the mostly consumed cake sitting on the coffee table.)* Would you like some?

KORBYN: Doesn't look like there's much left.

ZAMZAR: Yeah. Sorry. I got a little peckish there. Y'know, I thought you both would have been here much sooner.

KORBYN: Well, I was trying to be fashionably late. I didn't want to be the first one to show up to the party. You know how awkward that can be.

ZAMZAR: *(beat)* Not really, no.

KORBYN: Right.

ZAMZAR: So…

KORBYN: So, why's he looking for you and where is he looking?

ZAMZAR: I told him that we were throwing a party for him down at the park.

KORBYN: What?

ZAMZAR: Yeah. I told him to meet us at the picnic tables by the duck pond.

KORBYN: When?

ZAMZAR: *(checks his watch)* About two hours ago.

KORBYN: Are you serious? *(Zamzar goes in to his backpack and pulls out a handful of confetti.)*

ZAMZAR: Yeah! I got in here right after he left. I thought he'd head down there, see that no one was waiting for him, he'd come home and then… *(throws confetti)* surprise!

KORBYN: Oh my God.

ZAMZAR: It's a good thing he's taking so long to get back here. It gave you enough time to get here. Now we can surprise him together. *(Zamzar produces more confetti from his bag and offers it to Korbyn.)*

KORBYN: No! No no no! That's horrible!

ZAMZAR: What?

KORBYN: You trick this poor guy into leaving his place with the promise of a birthday party that no one's at, then you break into his apartment and invite a total stranger over so together we can scare the living hell out of him when he gets home?! Are you crazy?

ZAMZAR: Well, when you put it that way… this may not have been the best plan.

KORBYN: No! I don't think it was!

ZAMZAR: Don't worry. I'm sure it'll all work out.

KORBYN: Yeah, well I'm leaving.

ZAMZAR: But you'll miss the party!

KORBYN: I'm fine with that.

ZAMZAR: Come on now. How sad would it be for Strath to return home to find only one of us here to celebrate his birthday with him? I'm sure he's on his way back here now!

KORBYN: What if he's not? What if he's sitting alone at the picnic tables by the duck pond weeping bitter tears because you tricked him into believing that there was going to be a birthday party for him there?

ZAMZAR: But the party for him is here.

KORBYN: *(frustrated)* Oh dear God. He doesn't know that!

ZAMZAR: Of course he doesn't! That would ruin the surprise! *(beat. Korbyn seethes.)* Besides, I don't think he'd stay down there very long. Those ducks are very aggressive.

KORBYN: Oh?

ZAMZAR: Yeah! When I went down there to scout the place out for the quest, one of those big white ones with the really long necks came right at me.

KORBYN: A big white duck?

ZAMZAR: Yup! Really fierce bugger. That duck had more balls than a lot of people I know. Chased me back to my car and nipped at my heels the whole way.

KORBYN: I think you're talking about a goose.

ZAMZAR: Regardless, it was quite the nasty piece of work.

KORBYN: And you sent Strath down to where this thing lives?

ZAMZAR: Yes. *(beat)* Oh my God!

KORBYN: What?

ZAMZAR: That duck!

KORBYN: Goose.

ZAMZAR: Goose! What if it went after him? We should go down and check on him!

KORBYN: No, we shouldn't.

ZAMZAR: Why not? What if he's hurt?

KORBYN: I'm sure he's fine, goose or no goose. Besides, what if he gets back here after we leave? Then there's no party at the park and no surprise party for him here when he gets home. Double whammy.

ZAMZAR: You're right. Well, what if one of us stays here and waits while the other goes and looks for him?

KORBYN: That might work. Do you know what he looks like?

ZAMZAR: Yeah. He's a seven-foot-tall green orc in full Death Monger Plate Armor.

KORBYN: I mean in real life. Not his avatar.

ZAMZAR: Oh. *(beat)* No. Do you?

KORBYN: No. *(They both sit down on the couch, each deep in thought trying to figure out a plan.)*

ZAMZAR: I don't know what to do. He's over two hours late to his own birthday party.

KORBYN: Can we get in touch with him?

ZAMZAR: We can't ruin the surprise!

KORBYN: I think determining the condition of his health and well being right now is a little more important than preserving the veil of secrecy here.

ZAMZAR: But I worked so hard on planning this! *(Korbyn shoots Zamzar an incredulous look.)* What am I going to do? I just lead our leader into a death trap! Me! His most trusted lieutenant! He's out there, lost and alone. Without any support. No healers, no archers. Nothing. What if something happens to him? What would happen to the guild? I can just hear their judgment upon me now. "Et tu, Zamzar?"

KORBYN: I think you're going a little overboard there, dude. *(beat)* Just try calling him. I'm sure everything's fine.

ZAMZAR: Fine… *(pulls out his smart phone)* Hey, I just got an e-mail. *(beat)* It's from Strath!

KORBYN: Read it!

ZAMZAR: "Hey Paul-"

KORBYN: Who?

ZAMZAR: That's me.

KORBYN: Oh! Paul. Jason. Nice to meet you.

ZAMZAR: Likewise. *(They shake hands quickly and go back to reading Strath's e-mail.)* "Hey Paul, thanks for the invitation to hang out down at the park today. Sounds like a great time, but I'm not going to be able to make it. Some friends surprised me with a trip to Vegas this weekend for my birthday and we're headed there now. Hope you guys have fun! Watch out for those ducks – they're pretty mean. I'll see you guys back in game when I get home. Later, Chad (AKA Strath)." *(They both stare at the e-mail for a moment. Then-)* What an asshole.

KORBYN: Huh?

ZAMZAR: I sent him that invitation to the party in the park over a month ago! He just bailed on us two hours AFTER his party was supposed to start to go to Vegas!

KORBYN: Well, at least we know he's okay.

ZAMZAR: Screw that! He thinks he just ditched me down at the park with that goose!

KORBYN: That's messed up.

ZAMZAR: I can't believe I was actually worried about him.

KORBYN: Me neither. *(beat)* So, what do you want to do? *(Zamzar thinks for a moment, then he decisively grabs a plate and fork for Korbyn and serves him a piece of cake.)*

ZAMZAR: You ever play the game on a totally sweet rig with wireless controllers, a liquid-cooled hexa-core processor, four linked monitors and a dedicated high-speed line?

KORBYN: No…

ZAMZAR: There's a first time for everything. Come on. *(They head off towards Chad's Command Center. **Blackout**.)*

Props

Birthday Cake (Zamzar)

2 Plates (Zamzar, Korbyn)

2 Forks (Zamzar, Korbyn)

Knife (Zamzar)

Backpack (Zamzar)

2 Laptops (Zamzar)

Confetti (Zamzar)

Smart Phone (Zamzar)

Pink Hat Blues

Pink Hat Blues premiered on August 14th, 2011 as a part of Theatre Unleashed's 24-Hour Theatre Festival, *Planes, Trains & Automobiles*. It featured Liesl Jackson as Miri and David Orosz as Seth. Directed by David Chrzanowski. Stage Manager Erin Scott.

PINK HAT BLUES

Setting

"D" Train on the Boston T. Green Line. Present day.

Cast

AUTOMATED VOICE – *Male or female. Any age. Announces the subway stops. Could have Boston accent.*

MIRI – *Marketing Executive. "Wicked haahd co-oah Sawx fan." 20's-40's.*

SETH – *Job seeker. Pink hat. 20's-30's.*

Scene

At lights up, Miri stands stage C in front of two empty chairs, one hand holding on to a pantomimed guide rail above her, the other holding a newspaper. She's dressed professionally. Perhaps she's a banker? A briefcase sits at her feet. She's lost in her reading.

AUTOMATED VOICE: Now arriving, Longwood. *(Miri expertly sways with the car as it crawls to a halt. Beat. Seth steps up into the car. He's dressed professionally in a suit. He looks around for a seat, but can't find any. He manages to find some room and grabs a hold of the rail next to Miri. He's preoccupied.)* Next stop, Fenway. *(The train surges as it leaves the station. Seth is unprepared and bumps slightly into Miri.)*
SETH: Sorry. *(Miri looks up from her paper, long enough to give him a look, and goes back to reading.)* I said I was sorry. *(She ignores him. Silence. Miri reads. Seth continues to stand. He stares off into space. He starts humming to himself. After a moment, he notices that Miri has taken her eyes off the paper and is glaring at him. Caught, he stops humming. Her eyes dart back to the print.)*

AUTOMATED VOICE: Now entering, Fenway. *(Seth and Miri sway together as the car rolls to a stop. They get pushed together as everyone around them exits. After a moment, they look around and sit down, side by side. Miri's eyes are still glued to the news.)* Next stop, Kenmore Square. *(The silences continues. They sway together slightly as the car starts to move again. Finally-)*

SETH: Emptied out here real quick, last stop.

MIRI: *(not looking up)* Day game.

SETH: Hmm?

MIRI: Day game. Sox/Tigers.

SETH: Oh.

MIRI: Not a baseball fan, I take it?

SETH: Me? No, not really.

MIRI: Ah.

SETH: Well, kinda. I mean, I grew up around here. When you grow up around here, you learn to root for the Sox, right?

MIRI: No, you don't.

SETH: Not a baseball fan either?

MIRI: I'm not talking about me. I'm talking about you.

SETH: What about me?

MIRI: You just contradicted yourself.

SETH: No I didn't.

MIRI: You said you're from around here?

SETH: Yep. Born in Worcester.

MIRI: You a Yankees fan?

SETH: Hell no.

MIRI: Who plays first base for the Sox?

SETH: *(shrugs)* I don't know.

MIRI: Then you're not a Sox fan.

SETH: What?

MIRI: You never learned to be a Sox fan.

SETH: Sure I did. I go to games.

MIRI: Your parents from here?

SETH: Huh? Uh, no.

MIRI: Where they from?

SETH: Miami.

MIRI: Marlins country. Figures. No *real* baseball fans down there.

SETH: I go to games. I cheer for the Sox. I sing along to *Sweet Caroline*. *(beat)* I've got a Sox hat.

MIRI: Is it pink?

SETH: Huh? Uh. No, it's Blue. With a red "B." White trim around it.

MIRI: *(with a smirk)* It's Pink.

AUTOMATED VOICE: Now arriving, Kenmore Square. *(The car comes to a stop. Seth and Miri sway with it. Their conversation continues.)*

SETH: Why don't you believe me?

MIRI: When did you start following the Sox? 2004? '07?

SETH: I've always kind of followed them.

MIRI: "Kind of?" Heh. Oh, yeah. You're a Pink Hat.

SETH: What's a Pink Hat?

AUTOMATED VOICE: Next stop, Hynes Convention Center. *(The subway starts to move.)*

MIRI: Fair-weather fan? Bandwagon Jumper? Pink Hat.

SETH: Why are they Pink Hats?

MIRI: Because real fans don't buy pink Sox hats. They wear the real team colors. Fair weathers buy the pink hats because they think they're cute. Trendy. Not because they actually Believe.

SETH: I don't have a pink hat.

MIRI: But you are one. Do you see what I mean?

SETH: No.

MIRI: How can you consider yourself to be a Sox fan when you don't know anything about the them?

SETH: What do I need to know about them? They're the home team. When you go to a game, you cheer for the home team. You boo the visiting team. You drink your overpriced beer. You sing "Take Me Out to the Ballgame" and then you go home. That's it. That's what a fan does.

MIRI: No, that's not what a *real* fan does. A real fan doesn't own a pink hat.

SETH: I DON'T OWN A PINK HA-

MIRI: You know what a real Sox fan is? Someone who knows why *No, No Nannette* sucks and heard of Babe Ruth before he was a Yankee. They know about the Green Monster and the Pesky Pole. They know about the Splendid Splinter, Yaz, The Spaceman and Big Papi. A real fan knows about Bucky Fuckin'

Dent. They know what happened when Grady left Pedro in too long and Aaron Fuckin' Boone. A real fan is someone who dies a little inside whenever they hear "It gets through Buckner!" They know why Dave Roberts and Mike Lowell should never have to buy their own drinks in this town again and have beheld the miracle of Curt's Bloody Sock. A real fan loves Tessie, put up with "Manny being Manny," thinks the Yankees suck, can't stand Pink Hats and has Dirty Water flowing in their veins. A real fan knows their heritage and understands what it was to live with this team in the Spring and die with them in the Fall during those 86 Cursed years. That's a real Sox fan. *(Beat. Seth stares at her blankly.)* You have no idea what I'm talking about, do you?

SETH: *(beat)* It's not a pink hat. *(Miri rolls her eyes and goes back to her paper. Beat.)* What? *(Beat. Miri ignores him. Seth looks at her for a moment. Beat. He looks away. Goes back to fidgeting.)*

AUTOMATED VOICE: Now arriving, Hynes Convention Center. *(The car slows to a stop. Seth checks his watch, then looks up at the subway map over the car door. He's counting stops until his destination. Miri notices.)*

MIRI: Where you headed?

SETH: Government Center.

AUTOMATED VOICE: Next Stop, Copley Square. *(The train starts to move.)*

MIRI: Court date?

SETH: No. Job interview in the Financial District.

MIRI: Ah. Nervous?

SETH: Is it that obvious?

MIRI: A little.

SETH: Sorry.

MIRI: No big deal. What's it for?

SETH: Marketing job with a company called "FSG". Saw the ad on CraigsList.

AUTOMATED VOICE: Now arriving, Copley Square. *(The train comes to a halt.)*

MIRI: "FSG?"

SETH: Yeah, the ad wasn't too descriptive. When they called me, they didn't say much about the company. Just that they worked with high profile clients and that the work would be with a national brand.

MIRI: I see.

AUTOMATED VOICE: Next stop, Arlington. *(The train starts to move.)*

SETH: Yeah. I tried Googling them, but there are a lot of companies around here with those initials.

MIRI: Oh yeah?

SETH: Yeah. It's frustrating. In the end, I decided I'd roll the dice and find out who they are when I get there.

MIRI: Risky.

SETH: I know, right?

MIRI: Yeah. What time's your interview?

SETH: Two.

MIRI: It's one o'clock now.

SETH: Yeah, I like to be early.

MIRI: That's good, at least.

SETH: Yep. Thinking that once I get there, I can scout 'em out and learn what I can before they call me in.

MIRI: Good idea. *(beat)* So, why should FSG hire a Pink Hat like yourself?

SETH: Stop calling me a Pink Hat.

AUTOMATED VOICE: Now arriving, Arlington. *(The train slows and stops as they talk.)*

MIRI: You would rather I call you a fair-weather fan? A bandwagon jumper?

SETH: I don't care. Call me whatever you want.

MIRI: Fine, you're a fair-weather fan.

SETH: Fine.

MIRI: So, why would Fenway Sports Group want to hire a fair-weather fan?

SETH: Fenway Sports Gro- *(it clicks)* Oh shit. *(beat)* How do you kno-?

MIRI: Seth Rommel?

SETH: *(beat, warily)* Yeah?

MIRI: Miri Lawrence. Fenway Sports Group. Director of Marketing. *(beat)* You're my two o'clock. *(She turns back to her paper. Seth blanches. **Blackout.**)*

Props

Briefcase (Miri)

Newspaper (Miri)

Folder w/ Resume (Seth)

ABOUT THE PLAYWRIGHT

Gregory Crafts is a transplanted East Coaster and a multi-hyphenate creative artist residing in the Arts District of North Hollywood, CA with his soul mate and inspiration, Jenn and their two cats. Besides writing, his interests include acting, directing, producing, playing video games, 5k mud runs, competitive Tae Kwon Do, chess, seeing live theatre in L.A. and playing Texas Hold'Em. He is a founding member of Theatre Unleashed and proud to serve as its Managing Director. In what little free time he has, he enjoys playing *Dungeons & Dragons* with his friends and nurses an unhealthy obsession with the Boston Red Sox.

www.gregorycrafts.com

NOW IN PRINT

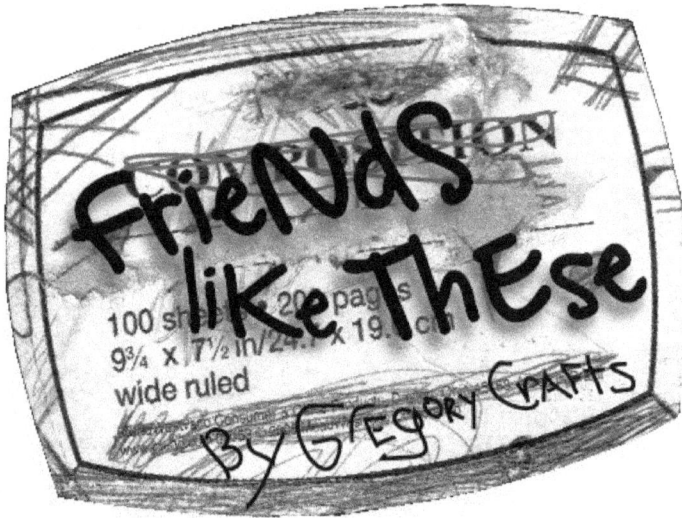

FRIENDS LIKE THESE

An original play by Gregory Crafts, *Friends Like These* takes a candid and poignant look at the staggering issue of violence in our high schools. Garrett is an outsider who spends most of his troubled existence in a fantasy world called Haven...that is until he meets Nicole, the popular cheerleader with a curious mind. As quickly as things begin looking up for Garrett, they come crashing down, forcing him to face both his past mistakes and his harsh present reality while he struggles for redemption. This gut-wrenching piece unswervingly explores the emotional trauma brought on by social mores during high school, forcing a confrontation with the causes and tragic consequences that left us staggered as a nation during Columbine and other high school shootings.

Format: Full Length
Genre: Drama
Duration: approx. 1hr. 45min.
Cast: 3 Male, 2 Female

www.friendsliketheseplay.com

www.ingramcontent.com/pod-product-compliance
Lightning Source LLC
LaVergne TN
LVHW091207080426
835509LV00006B/874